A Lifetime of Sisters Weekends

Copyright © 2023 by Linda Silva

All rights reserved. This book or any portion thereof may not be reproduced or used in any manner whatsoever without the express written permission of the publisher except for the use of brief quotations in a book review.

Printed in the United States of America

First Printing, 2023

ISBN-13: 9-79-8-3729777-4-7

A Lifetime of Sisters Weekends

Linda Silva

with

Diane Mota, Elaine Montgomery, Michelle White,
Dolores Ouimet, Susan Roy, and Marianne O'Brien

This book is dedicated to our parents, Paul Ethier Sr. and Loretta (Bell) Ethier, and our three brothers: Paul Jr., Richard, and Mederic.

January 1, 1997; Two months before our father's passing.
Top: Linda, Dolores, Mederic, Richard, Paul, Michelle, Susan, Marianne.
Bottom: Diane, Loretta (Mom), Paul (Dad), Elaine.

May 2, 2022, Cancun Mexico
Our first whole-family vacation ever.
Bottom: Dolores, Diane, Susan, Michelle, Marianne, Linda, Elaine. Top: Mederic, Paul, Richard.

Contents

The Sisters ... 1
- Some Background ... 1
- Family History ... 3
- Addiction and Dysfunction ... 4
- How It All Started ... 6
- The Weekends ... 7
- Tension and Triggers ... 14
- Trauma, Memories, and Growth ... 17
- Labels ... 19
- How to Become Emotionally Aware ... 20

Our Stories ... 24
- Susan's Story ... 24
- Diane's Story ... 26
- Elaine's Story ... 28
- Michelle's Story ... 31
- Marianne's Story ... 35
- Linda's Story ... 37
- Dolores's Story ... 39
- Mom's Story ... 42
- Mom and Dad ... 43
- Where We Are Today ... 45

Your Weekends ... 48
- Let's Sort It Out ... 49
- Emotional Preparedness ... 50
- What We Learned and How You Can Prepare ... 51
- Two Questions to Ask Yourself ... 52
- Becoming Aware/More Questions ... 53

The Journey ... 54
Recommended Reading: ... 55

The Sisters

This guide is not meant only for sisters. It's meant for anyone who wants to learn how to grow, develop strong bonds, and learn to love themselves by way of an annual gathering. The intent is to empower other women to grow and support one another as they become better versions of themselves. Let's make this world better by learning to love ourselves and each other. Welcome to *A Lifetime of Sisters Weekends*. Thank you for joining our journey.

Let me introduce my sisters, oldest to youngest: Diane, Elaine, Michelle, Dolores, Susan, and Marianne. My name is Linda, the author and fifth sister of the family. There would be no story without the life experiences and contributions from my sisters.

Some Background

Years ago, we had a ghostwriter begin drafting a book about our sisters weekends. All seven of us collaborated and provided stories for the chapters. Eventually we started getting triggered again and figured out that we were not quite ready to share our journey. There were arguments over the accuracy of the events. What I found interesting is, although the memories were accurate, the stories differed between the sisters based on the reactions we each experienced. We decided we needed to put the book on pause. You see, we all knew it would make a great story someday, but at that time we were not emotionally prepared to make it happen. That's when we learned to appreciate that this is a journey, not a destination.

In 2021, Elaine joined us again after a ten-year hiatus. She had been on her own healing journey. Our journey, though incomplete, had come full circle. We were all able to attend a sisters weekend without the fears that used to control us. We were joined together by fate, not by choice. The choice we made was to cultivate our relationships to fulfill our desires to heal as individuals and as a collective. The drama was real, and the lessons learned are universal.

It was thirty-seven years after our first adventure when I decided it was time to write a book about our annual sisters weekends. (We have celebrated year thirty-eight since the start of writing this book.) The idea started as a how-to book, but it has grown into more than that. The journey from our heads to our hearts is the longest journey there is. We have been on this journey since we were born, our lifetime as sisters.

This book is more about how we were able to continue our weekend getaway tradition despite sometimes not wanting to go for one reason or another. Some sisters were afraid of being triggered by the others, some sisters took on the challenge, while others just came along for the ride. Another recurring issue was the fear of being away from family for too long, leaving our children with our husbands, or both. The bottom line is that the discomfort could have deterred us from growing or co-creating together, but we were able to keep our focus on the goal of authentic healing—despite the triggers.

Often, on a sisters weekend, someone would get triggered and have overwhelming feelings of inferiority, jealousy, embarrassment, or shame (to name just a few) that wreaked havoc on the mind and body. The emotions could be so strong that they affected our ability to interact or participate on parts of the weekend.

Our emotions are our teachers. They are streams of energy that allow us to express ourselves. Becoming aware of what each emotion feels like, where it is in our bodies, and how we react to it is the work required to understand ourselves. It is not always appropriate to act on an emotion. You see, emotions arise from the subconscious to give us information about a life situation. Your experiences and how you interpret them depends on how you react to a given situation. So, not everyone reacts to every situation the same. Most people have been trained to suppress, ignore, or repress their emotions. Thus, not aware of them most or all their lives. Or they may label them but don't really feel them. Then try to justify their emotions by blaming or explaining. So, nothing changes.

Over the years, we have developed our own emotional awarenesses, and still are working on it today. It can be difficult to show the changes as they occurred over the years because it's an extensive timeline and there are so many sisters that it can get messy. To help explain, I have added some stories that were written by each sister to provide more perspective and details.

It is my hope that sharing our story will help others realize the effects trauma has on people and how it manifests differently for everyone. But more importantly, I want people to know there is a way out. By using the tools presented, you, too, can learn how to overcome the effects of trauma and negative experiences to create healthier relationships with anyone you choose.

The techniques in this book can be used without other people having to change. First, you must commit to learning about yourself. All relationships take some form of commitment and effort, and it all begins with you.

The tools shared in this book are from various sources I have learned from along the way. You may need to seek professional support during your own healing.

Family History

For you to fully understand why it was sometimes difficult to be together, I need to cover some family history.

We were raised in Mansfield, MA; twelve people in a five bedroom, one-and-a-half bath house. We were a blue-collar family with a lot of dysfunctions. At times, it was so chaotic and traumatic that we lost the ability to trust or love one another. Dad was an alcoholic and Mom had to go to work, which left us to fend for ourselves and care for each other. Although there are many great memories, there are many painful ones as well. These dysfunctional experiences created behaviors and patterns in each of us. Survival techniques. These became so familiar that we didn't realize they were a problem until we started reacting to each other, on our weekends, in an unhealthy way.

However, we kept working on our relationships because it was the ultimate gift we could give ourselves. We went from superficial relationships to ones built on love and trust. We are seven sisters who never really complained about our pasts, nor were we bitter. We accepted it for what it was. We each found our way in the world, with our own families and full lives. We could have easily moved on from the old memories and grown apart, but instead we chose to find a way to stay connected. We did that through our annual sisters weekends.

Addiction and Dysfunction

Early on, we didn't know what a trigger was or why we were triggered. Everyone has different experiences in life and different interpretations of those experiences. If you asked siblings in any family, "How was your upbringing?" their answers would probably be different from each other, regardless of socioeconomic status. That is what happened in our family too. Birth order played a role, personality played a role, and gender played a role. Growing up in the '50s, '60s, and '70s, men were taught to be tough and not feel their emotions while women wore their emotions on their sleeves. In our family, this is how it was. I expressed my emotions whether it was sadness or anger. I would kick and scream or withdraw to my room to indulge my feelings.

Dad started drinking in the Army, before he married our mother, and his drinking was the primary source of our traumas. He would get angry and sometimes even violent when he was drunk. Everyone was afraid of him—except Diane, the oldest. She would put him in his place every chance she could. Many times, he would play Hank Williams and Johnny Cash songs on repeat all night long. We didn't get much sleep those nights. I remember lying in bed wishing he would stop. I'm sure I wasn't alone in feeling that way.

Our mother started working outside the home after my last sibling was born. She had to work to keep us fed and with a roof over our head. Dolores recalls the many times the phone would ring in the afternoon, and she knew it was mom calling to say she would be working a double. My heart would sink, knowing she wouldn't be coming home until after we were in bed.

There were different forms of physical and emotional abuse in our house, from our parents and each other. Frustration was a common emotion between us. We were all in survival mode. Our basic needs—like being nurtured, having enough food, feeling safe, and even sleep—were not always met.

Addiction affects everyone in the family, whether it is known at the time or not. An addict can be abusive physically and emotionally, knowingly or unknowingly, aware or unaware—it does not matter. My father took out his frustrations on the older kids and my mom. Yet, the younger kids were not unscathed by his behaviors. The effects of that unhealed childhood trauma is what we sisters have been working on. We were not clear, until recently that this is what has caused our pettiness, frustrations, and the like. Here are a few examples of what we were trying to heal from:

- Codependency
- Not being able to prioritize our own needs
- Living on high alert
- Trying to fix others
- Need for external validation
- People-pleasing
- Enabling

I wish I understood back then what I was trying to heal. Codependency was something we were all familiar with from our exposure to Alcoholics Anonymous, Al-Anon, and Alateen, but I was not fully aware of the other behaviors that had been controlling me for so long. Looking back, I can see how I had all these unhealthy behaviors from which I struggled to find a way to heal.

Our stories reflect our behaviors and reactions to simple things while on our weekends. (See Dolores's and Susan's stories.) The reactions can be strong enough to dissolve relationships if they are not transformed.

We had to learn in our adult years what functional families learn in their childhoods. Some sisters went on to other abusive relationships in their adult lives, which created a longer healing journey. (See Elaine's story.) The stories we share about our sisters weekends are examples of our own thoughts, feelings, and conflicts to help you understand how these factored into our interactions with each other.

We did better when we knew better, but first we had to realize that we were worthy of better lives and that it was possible to have them. That took time.

How It All Started

It began in 1985, when seven sisters set out on a weekend away with their sister-in-law, who had just lost one of her own. Two cars, eight women, and a reservation at the Best Western in New Hampshire. My sister-in-law, Kathy, and I were pregnant. Susan and Marianne, who were twenty and eighteen respectively, weren't even old enough to drink. We had no idea what to expect or how it would go. All we knew was that we wanted to have fun and connect as sisters.

We are a family of ten siblings—seven girls and three boys. There is a thirteen-year age gap between the eldest, Diane, and the youngest, Marianne. Diane and Elaine are a year and a day apart. Due to when our brothers were born, growing up, Michelle did not have a sister close to her age. Because of this, she had to develop her relationship with each of us throughout the years. She wanted everyone to have the same experience, so she suggested we have a sisters weekend. We all replied with enthusiasm: we were in. A little uncertain, for sure, but in. (See Michelle's story.)

Diane and Elaine both moved out of our house when they were seventeen, a year apart from each other. Marianne was only four years old when Diane got married and moved out. Our relationships with the older sisters were different from with those still living at home. After all, we still shared our clothes and a bedroom with each other. That's another story!

Speaking of age differences, I should note that the two oldest sisters were like our mothers until that point. They took care of us younger kids, even after they moved out. We were ready to take that responsibility away from them and prove to them we could take care of ourselves. It was time to change our relationship dynamic from caregivers to sisters. (Read Diane's story.)

That first year we hit Hampton Beach, NH. It had a boardwalk jam-packed with souvenir shops, bars, restaurants, hotels, and, of course, the beach! We were all thick in the throes of '80s fashion, sporting the big sunglasses, permed hair, and padded shoulders. We walked the boardwalk, looked in the shops, ate dough boys covered in chocolate sauce, and went to a great restaurant with outdoor seating where we ordered lobsters and steamers. There were picnic tables to sit at, and we ate our lobsters and steamed clams as melted butter dripped down our arms, enjoying every bite. Diane was the one who loved lobster most and she ate whatever we didn't have the patience for. She would retrieve the meat from the little legs and anything else she could get her hands on. We enjoyed watching her indulge in the delicacy. There were a lot of laughs! We also spent a good deal of time in the hotel room. It was fun trying to get a group photo of us all sitting on the bed using the timer on my camera. Getting everyone in the picture was no easy task!

I don't think we knew it was going to be an annual event at the time. We enjoyed our first adventure so much that we decided to continue with the getaways—and never looked back. Getting together as sisters gave us the opportunity to share decorating ideas and recipes, shop together, get creative, be silly, and create a safe place to share and ultimately heal our wounds.

1985 - Hampton Beach, New Hampshire
Top: Dolores, Linda, Susan. Bottom: Kathy (SIL), Marianne, Elaine, Diane, Michelle.

The Weekends

As the tradition continued, not everyone attended. Dolores missed the second year's trip because she was pregnant and needed bed rest and we couldn't reschedule. This is how we stayed the course for the last thirty-eight years. Elaine missed many weekends over the years as well. We wanted her to come, and I know she wanted to be there, but we triggered her in ways that none of us understood at the time, including her. (See Elaine's story.) That did not deter us from continuing the tradition. We wanted to continue to grow and bond, to learn to love unconditionally and accept the things we could not change.

That was the commitment we made to ourselves. Our journey to self-revelation, self-awareness, and self-preservation. No matter how painful it was sometimes to be together, we had fun, experimented, got creative, and supported one another.

Whenever we gathered as a family for holidays and birthday parties, the collection of sisters, kids, and husbands produced such a large group. There was never enough time to catch up or talk about what we wanted to talk about. And that has only gotten truer. Nowadays, there are twenty-three grandchildren, twenty-eight great-grandchildren, and one great-great-grandchild—not to mention the sisters-in-law and brothers-in-law. Yikes!

As we committed to this venture, some of our husbands were not totally on board. There were small children at home, responsibilities that felt unmanageable to them etc. That did not deter us. Over the years their perspective changed as they noticed the positive impact after we returned from our weekend. Of course, the children were easier to take care of as well. (Read Marianne's Story) One year the husbands planned their own little getaway, but that was short lived.

The Today Show, New York City 2000
Diane, Michelle, Linda, Elaine, Dolores, Susan, and Marianne (Some of us wearing our dwarf sweatshirts)

One year, we took a limousine to New York City to see *Phantom of The Opera*, which most of my sisters and I slept through. We were seen on *The Today Show* and took a walk-in central park, but my all-time favorite was eating at a restaurant in Little Italy. The restaurant walls were decorated with pictures of customers from over the years and the tables were packed together. I think the spirits were as high as the noise level! I don't remember a menu, but the server brought one course after another, family style, all while the wine bottles were replenished as soon as they were emptied. We enjoyed every bite, but the taxi ride to and from was another story.

On our third trip to Hampton Beach, New Hampshire, we recorded a dance video (on VHS) to the popular song "Girls Just Wanna Have Fun" by Cindy Lauper. It ended up being our theme song for many years. Another time, we went white water rafting on a not-so-rough river in New Hampshire. We've gone to so many plays, but my favorite is the production of *The Wizard of Oz* we saw in a small playhouse in Foxboro, MA. The simplicity of the set and costumes enhanced the performance by the actors and actresses. There was a picnic in Maine, a limousine ride to Boston to see the *Vagina Monologues*, and stopping for lobster rolls at a small oceanside restaurant. We've had so many luncheons, walks on the beach, spa treatments, and so much more.

The celebrations were countless. We celebrated our birthdays almost every year with cake and gifts. One year, we celebrated Michelle's college graduation, which fell on a sisters weekend, with a graduation ceremony. We all wore caps and gowns and received handmade diplomas based on our characteristics. Another year, we had a baby shower for Marianne and a wedding shower for Elaine (which she missed because she didn't come that year). We walked and we talked, we laughed and we cried, we sang and we danced, we dined and we shined. Our weekends would not be the same without the fairy dust Diane brought. There was nothing dull about our weekends. Christmas in July, concerts, pottery making, swimming, and, of course, shopping and cooking.

Diane loves to bring things to our weekends. We never know what to expect from her. She packs more than we could ever imagine or fit in the trunks of our cars. Elaine always likes to write us letters and inspire us in some way and has brightened our weekends with her endless love and humor. Michelle loves to plan the getaways for us. Without her, we wouldn't be doing these or the other family vacations she's planned over the years. Dolores is a great organizer and cook. She pulls together meals like a professional chef—simple, but delicious. I like to bring pictures from our previous trips and place them around the house we stay at. Having them reminds us of where we were and how far we've come. Susan has always brought her calm, positive presence, and now she brings more creativity and laughter, which sparks joy in everyone. Marianne brings her organizational skills and her huge heart. She loves and appreciates everything on our weekends.

Year five was pivotal for us. It was the most tumultuous weekend thus far. We stayed in two hotel rooms in Cape Cod, Massachusetts while trying to keep cost as low as we could. I'm not sure if we really needed to, but we were conditioned to be frugal by a childhood of little means. We were always told we couldn't afford things, so I don't think we sought other options. Everyone's emotions were high all weekend. There was a lot of drama, fear, chaos, and confusion on everyone's part. (See Diane's story.) I remember Susan and me saying on the drive home that we were not going to go the next year. I believe we all felt that way at the time. However, when it came time for the next weekend, year six, we all attended yet again! We kept going back because we needed to prove to ourselves that we were stronger than the addiction that raised us and the fears that controlled us.

We had the sixth year of our sisters weekends in 1990. Susan had just had her first child and was nursing, so Elaine invited us to her house for the weekend so the baby could come too. This was our first sisters weekend at someone's house. I was seven months pregnant with my third child. Elaine was an amazing hostess. She had red carnations and baby's breath in vases with red ribbons for each of us on her kitchen table. We had a plethora of food, and the tranquil atmosphere made the weekend more relaxed than the previous one. Since we weren't going out, we had fortune tellers come to the house for entertainment purposes. That added drama, but not on our part. They told my sister Diane that if she paid them $200, they would light a candle to ward off all the "bad" things happening in her life. She cried because she didn't have the money to give them. It was a scam, but it took hours for us to shift Diane's energy and talk about everything they told us. We swam in Elaine's pool and just relaxed that weekend. The highlight of the weekend was getting the baby to laugh for the first time, surrounded by the love of his Aunties.

That was the year we realized that staying in a house was better than staying in hotel rooms; the added common areas and outdoor space really allowed us to spread out a bit and relax. This was before Airbnb existed, which has made it easier since then.

What kept us going back? A strong connection. It was all part of the journey. We had *needed* each other when we were children, but now we *chose* each other.

On our twenty-first trip, we attended a sponsored sisters weekend in St. Charles, Illinois, where Dolores lived. This event included the pajama party featured on the cover of this book, a wine-and-cheese reception, a bingo bash, a spa treatment, dance workshops, yoga, a fashion show, a treasure hunt, and more. The folks running the event told us during the application process that they'd never had a large group of actual sisters, so they were excited to meet us. We were featured in the local newspapers of both St. Charles and our hometown of Mansfield, Massachusetts. The mayor of St. Charles was interested in meeting us as well. She found us on the first evening and invited us to her office the following day to get to know us better and give Dolores a key to the city as a token.

Whenever we were back at Dolores's house, we were pampered by her husband. Appetizers were served, wine was poured, and a fire crackled in the fireplace as we gathered around to chat. We had a multitude of adventures, from shopping in Chicago to the events in St. Charles, to gift giving, and (as always) sharing updates on our lives with each other. We ended the weekend with a limousine ride to the airport. The hard part was leaving Dolores in St. Charles. Saying goodbye is always difficult for the sister who's left behind—in this case, Dolores.

There were some moments during this weekend that there were triggers. While we were attending an event at an old theater downtown, two local radio hosts, Kathy and Judy, were going to "share their wit and wisdom on their own brand of sisterhood." Later, I found out that most of us hadn't wanted to attend this event and would rather have stayed at Dolores's house to sit by the fire and enjoy our last evening together. But no one spoke up, so we went—only to be disappointed by the show. It wasn't a comedy show like we'd thought. At some point, the event coordinator told us that the hosts were going to ask us a question as part of their show. Dolores jumped up and waved her hands in the air when the hosts asked if we were in the audience, which embarrassed Diane. She tried to shush Dolores and keep her from making a scene. This may seem petty to some people, but when you're not aware that this reaction comes from old patterns and trauma, the feeling is strong and painful. It washes over you just like a fit of anger would.

Any emotion can feel overwhelming and cause a reaction that is not in line with the situation. Once this feeling floods through you, how do you control it? It can be difficult to shake off. A typical response to being triggered is to try to justify the reaction. Then you may start creating a story about the person who triggered you: "She always does that, she's so obnoxious, what is wrong with her?" Things we've all said to ourselves when triggered.

Fortunately, we were able to draw from our experiences and get through those triggers. How I managed was to focus on my own emotions. Doing this created less drama by not feeding into whatever Diane was feeling, by holding a safe space for feelings to be felt, and by understanding the process.

Healing is done through emotional awareness. The key to emotional awareness is to notice the emotion by feeling it. You can label it if you want to—anger, sadness, fear, happiness, and so on. Take a moment to pause, breathe, and feel. When you do this, you're allowing yourself to be aware of what's going on inside you. I don't know if Diane was able to connect with her embarrassment at that point, but I do know I was more aware of my emotions to just stay present. That diverted more drama, which is the goal on these weekends.

We celebrated our twenty-fifth sisters weekend in Plymouth, Massachusetts at Dolores's beach house in 2009. Our silver anniversary! We paired up and did skits for each other. Diane and Elaine dressed in silver, head to toe, and sang a song to the tune of "Silver Bells." Here are the lyrics they wrote:

> Christmas makes us feel emotional
> It may bring parties or thoughts devotional
> Whatever happens or what may be,
> Here is what sister weekends mean to me.

The Sisters

Silver Bells

City sidewalk, country sidewalks
Dressed in New York City style,
In the air there's a feeling of sisters weekend.
Sisters laughing, people passing,
Meeting smile after smile,
And on every street corner you'll hear:
25 years, 25 years,
It's our time… in Plymouth.
Ring-a-ling, hear them ring, (Throw Confetti)
Soon it will be here again.
City streetlights,
Even stop lights,
Blink of bright red and green,
As the sisters rush home with their treasures.
Hear the husbands crunch,
See the kids bunch,
This is sisters big scene,
And above all this bustle you'll hear:
25 years, 25 years,
It's sisters time in the city.
Ring-a-ling, hear them ring, (Throw Confetti)
Soon it will be fifty years!

A Lifetime of Sisters Weekends

Michelle, Susan, and Marianne dressed in top hats and canes and choreographed dances to our "theme songs" from over the years: "Girls Just Wanna Have Fun," "Two Pina Coladas," and "New York, New York." Then they planned the after-party, with appetizers and Dom Perignon.

I paired up with Dolores. We dressed in silver, very similar to Diane and Elaine's costumes—unbeknownst to us. We made up a song as well, then played a trivia game about our sisters weekends with prizes for the winners. It was an amazing time with all stellar performances!

Sisters Weekend Year 25, 2009
Left: Marianne, Michelle, and Susan.
Above: Linda, Elane, Dolores, and Diane.

The themes always brought our focus to the intent of the getaway. These weekends helped us connect to our artistic sides and be creative with one another, while building new memories to cherish.

Tension and Triggers

The growth we experienced was an effect of the tensions and triggers we dealt with on our weekends. This is how it went:

The drama started in year one. By year five, we were squirting water guns at each other to vent our frustrations, talking behind each other's backs, and declaring we would never go on these trips again. I had a little black box that said four different phrases whenever I pressed its button: "eat shit," "eff you," "you're an a-hole," and "effing jerk!" Whenever a sister got on my nerves (triggered me), I would go right up to her and press the button repeatedly. It released my pent-up tension and made us laugh, for the most part.

Some sisters did not think it was funny.

There were plenty of painful moments when we were playing the blame games or judging each other. Blaming and looking outside ourselves were coping mechanisms to help us feel more in control. We never addressed the issues with the person who triggered us, only talked behind their back with another sister who would agree with us. What we did not know was that each of us had emotions brewing inside: unworthiness, anxiety over conflict, insecurities, shame, guilt, jealousy, and more. It didn't have anything to do with the other sisters, but we didn't know that then. The painful emotions were inside of each of us, waiting for something or someone to trigger it. We were emotionally unaware. (See Diane's and Elaine's stories.)

The tensions would build over the weekend if we didn't take responsibility for them. (See Elaine's and Dolores's stories.) It was difficult to see the frustration and callousness over a reaction to someone saying or doing the "wrong thing" or jealousy of another sister's wealth, flamboyance, or beliefs. We took everything so personally! Some sisters showed their anger and fear while others sat back, watched, and held it inside.

Our father had a favorite prayer that helped us understand the need to let go and accept ourselves and each other:

> *"God grant me the serenity, to accept the things I cannot change, Courage to change the things I can and the Wisdom to know the difference."*
> —Reinhold Niebuhr

We learned that unless we were willing to also "practice" that acceptance with each other, the prayer was just words. Until this new version of the serenity prayer was written with more clarity:

> *"God grant me the serenity to accept the people I cannot change, the courage to change the one I can, and the wisdom to know it's me."*
> —Father James Martin

I love this version. It has helped me to keep the focus on my own healing inward, not outward. It was me that had to change, and that I did.

As we moved toward our goal to love unconditionally, stay connected, and heal, we kept working on ourselves the best we could. The weekends continued with or without a sister. We had to face our own jealousy, judgments, and anger—along with our husbands' reactions as we hauled off for a getaway and left them with the kids. (See Marianne's story.) As we learned to understand our emotions, we were able to enjoy the process and the weekends more.

The first twenty years or so, there was always something that set one of us off. I remember one weekend we stayed at Elaine's house and attended her Sunday morning church service. Dolores had a sister-in-law who was in cancer treatment, and she needed to call her about something when the service was scheduled to begin. I suggested she call fifteen minutes early to avoid being late for church, but in Dolores's mind, that wasn't possible. She felt she needed to respect the time she and her sister-in-law had agreed on and would not budge, mad that I even suggested it. I responded with anger and confusion and distanced myself from her as I processed our reactions. It made no sense to me that she couldn't call a few minutes early.

This type of behavior comes from something that was taught to us as children: fear of disrespecting someone. Respect was the utmost value that our parents ingrained in us. That is what they were taught by their parents, to a fault. This meant that we gave our power away to others. We had respect for others and their feelings but not for ourselves. That is why we were mistreated later in our lives. We did not speak up for ourselves; if we tried, we were punished.

This was a hard dynamic to reverse. We needed to learn how to be respectful to others while not disrespecting our own values at the same time. We needed to learn how to love and respect ourselves. That was and still can be a challenge.

Our sisters weekends had many different triggers. Take the aerosol hairspray incident in year five, for example. Dolores was concerned about the environment and complained about the rest of us using aerosol hairspray. She harped on it all weekend while the rest of us were hoping she would "get over it."

That same weekend, Michelle was in the hotel room ironing her clothes in her underwear. Unaware of this, Dolores opened the door just as people were walking by—not once, but twice! Michelle reacted with, "Shut the effing door!" Again, more gossiping and more painful emotions. Shame and guilt.

Jealousy was always a trigger (who looked better than who, who bought new clothes for the weekend, and so on) but there was no shortage of others: what someone said or did, practical jokes, fear of triggering other sisters, or being judged or blamed for something.

Here's the thing about being triggered: you must not blame the person that triggered you. Look at yourself instead. It took us many years to learn we were being triggered and how to identify it. Gradually, through different avenues, we started to discover how to stop the emotional rollercoaster. These emotional rides were not just on sisters weekends, but in all areas of our lives. They were the reason we decided to learn more about ourselves and to seek healing and happiness.

Trauma, Memories, and Growth

As I write this book, I learn even more about triggers and the behaviors behind them. The triggers we experienced were based on our traumas. Most people have experienced trauma as a child or even as an adult. Everyone lives their lives based on their experiences and their interpretations of those experiences or traumas. We were not aware that we were reacting to traumatic experiences. Not until the patterns of behavior became so disruptive to our relationships that we wanted to understand and grow from them. That's when we realized we have a choice. A choice to nurture our wounds.

> *"Trauma comes back as a reaction, not a memory."*
> —Bessel Van Der Kolk

This quote changed my perspective of trauma. I still have reactions from my childhood traumas. I do so without reliving the memory of the trauma itself, but it's a feeling that overwhelms and tries to control me. I don't like labels, but I would say the reactions I have are feelings of anxiety or Post Traumatic Stress Disorder.

As I become more and more aware of these feelings, I can catch them more quickly when they arise. I stay focused on the healing and the feeling, not the trauma. The emotions can be so strong that it feels like the "shame" of the trauma is happening now. I must sit with it and feel the pain for a while until I stop reacting, as I try not to believe the thoughts associated with the feelings. Those imaginary thoughts add fuel to the fire of these painful sensations and only serve to create more misery. The type of trauma doesn't matter, the healing process is the same; you must feel it to heal it.

I have been on a path of healing for over three decades. The year I turned thirty, I wanted to let go of a secret I'd been hiding for twenty-five years: I had been abused by neighbors as a child. I was afraid to tell anyone about it, but the older I got the harder it became to hold in. It took an emotional breakdown for me to get help. Once I started my healing journey, I told Dolores my secret and then my parents. It was so hard to say it out loud; I felt so much shame. This secret was holding me back from my self-worth and my self-confidence. I needed to heal the past so I could learn to be in the present. I wanted to be a better mother and wife. Ultimately, I had to learn to forgive so I could be free.

On the next sisters weekend, I decided to share with the rest of my sisters. There were several reasons behind my decision. First, for the support. Second, to help with my healing process as I attempted to let go of the shame and guilt. Third, to allow others to be open and vulnerable about childhood traumas if they had any to share.

The support from my sisters varied. Some were uncomfortable with the news, others wanted to help me by talking about it. Some started sharing their own traumas, while others weren't ready quite yet.

Sharing my abuse was one of the hardest things I've done. So many people suffer in silence. They are not ready to feel the pain of their trauma and hope it will go away someday. Thats what I'd hoped, too, but it didn't work for me.

Some sisters had different traumas in their childhood. Those left scars as well, which led to distrust, insecurities, and blame. The triggers we experienced on our sister weekends were born mostly from those traumas. They made our home lives tumultuous while growing up and later when we started our own families. Although Mom and Dad did the best they could, it wasn't always good enough. We basically raised ourselves with the help of the older siblings. We all fought a lot.

Our sisters weekends brought these issues out. We'd wonder so many things. "Why is she so angry?" "Who does she think she is?" "Why does she bring so much stuff?" "Why doesn't she talk to us?" "I can't stand it when she acts that way!" We just didn't know what we didn't know.

And so, the growing began. Allowing myself to be vulnerable was a good start. We learned from each other and shared what we learned whenever appropriate. We're still growing and practicing today.

Labels

We each had labels growing up, such as "black sheep," "baby of the family," "sensitive," "shy," and "twiggy." One weekend, we even labeled ourselves the Seven Dwarves and took names based on our childhood personalities—or our perceptions of them. I was Sleepy because I liked to take naps. Truth be told, however, I was just scared and depressed during that part of my childhood, and naps were a way to escape from the world and my pain. Elaine was Grumpy. She didn't think she deserved that label, but someone had to have it. She was given Grumpy because when we were little, she always kept us in line at the house and made us do our chores. Naturally, we did not like it; we thought she was being mean.

When we label ourselves or others, we put them in a box. This identifier is likely inaccurate and restrictive. Our minds like to cling to these labels as if they're truth. Thus, repeatedly labeling someone as "shy" or "mean" keeps that person shy or mean.

Letting go of the labels is important for families and ourselves. Letting go frees a person from a perspective that may not be true anymore—and possibly never was. The example of my sister Elaine shows this very well. Her label was far from true. She's not "Grumpy." In fact, she's pretty "Happy" now.

Let go of labels! (See Susan's story.)

How to Become Emotionally Aware

First, you need to become aware of your emotions.

Emotions are produced in the conscious and unconscious mind, while feelings are both physical sensations and emotional experiences which arise from our conscious state of being. Trauma has a great impact on our emotions, often causing stress, anxiety, anger, sadness, shame, and guilt—thus, triggering painful feelings.

Painful feelings and emotions create our reactions, such as bouts of anger or isolation. The key is to notice them in your body. They come as a physical sensation. Painful physical sensations usually present as tightness, sharpness, nausea, or throbbing in different areas of your body, most commonly the chest, head, throat, or abdomen. These physical sensations are warnings that you have been triggered. Usually, the triggers are based on your thoughts or beliefs about something someone said or did, or even a story you created around a situation based on your beliefs or a trauma. (See Linda's and Dolores's stories.)

How aware are you of your thoughts? Did you know that you have some control over them? You can change the way you think, which in turn changes the way you feel and ultimately the way you act or react. When you notice the physical sensation(s), you can choose either to react by shouting or withdrawing or to sit with the feeling and accept it as your own. As you sit and feel it, notice the thoughts that go along with it. This can take a few minutes or longer. If you decide to wait, you'll be able to respond to the situation instead of reacting to it.

This is where your power lies. The moment you notice what you are feeling, find the thoughts that are triggering the feeling, and choose what you're going to do next. You feel powerless when you're angry, jealous, or judgmental. (See Linda's story.) But you have all the power in the world if you take notice of what's happening in your body and mind in that moment. You do have a choice: the decision to feel. Avoiding the painful emotions is not an option for me anymore. Let alone trying to avoid them by shouting, eating, drinking, shopping, or blaming.

There's an old Native American parable about how everyone has two wolves fight going on inside of them. The wolves represent the two sides everyone has: the angry, superior, and egotistical side, and the loving, kind, generous, and compassionate side. The grandson of the Cherokee asked his grandfather, "Which wolf will win the fight?" His grandfather replied, "Whichever wolf you feed." It's ultimately your choice, and that choice will result in either a loving relationship or a disconnected one. Which wolf are you are you going to feed?

If we are emotionally unaware, we can create a threshold event. For example: when we argue with a spouse, coworker, or someone else and it's left unnoticed, we carry those feelings around with us all day. Then we have something else that triggers us, and so on, and so on. We end up in full-blown trigger mode and blame the nearest person for something that happened with someone else long before. Painful emotions on top of painful emotions that went unnoticed.

Emotional awareness can prevent drama, threshold events, and more painful emotions. It can help you heal from the inside out. Be mindful of the initial trigger. Take responsibility for it. Instead of reacting, respond in the best way you can, without judging yourself or the other person. Start by feeling it. Are you willing to feel uncomfortable? That's the ultimate question because of how uncomfortable it is to feel painful sensations in our bodies.

On our sisters weekends, we would do a lot of blaming to avoid taking responsibility for our own emotions. When you blame someone for how you're feeling, you're looking in the wrong direction. Blame comes from fear. If I blame someone for how I feel, I'm basically giving away my power. I'm saying they can control my emotions. When you're no longer reactive, you can evaluate the situation with clarity and keep yourself from overreacting. In turn, this will help stop your chaos and drama. The only control you have is over yourself.

When you can, just sit and feel the painful emotions in your body. Observe them without judgment. As I said before, it's important to also pay attention to what you are thinking. Are you creating a story about the situation in your mind? Justifying your reaction? Instead, just sit and feel. It's uncomfortable at first, but it allows you to process painful emotions without reacting. It's important to remember that it is just a feeling or uncovered emotion—physical sensations in your body, nothing more and nothing less. Try not to judge the sensations as good or bad. They're just sensations. It takes time to feel them. The more you feel and recognize them, the less hold they will have over you. Again, this requires practice. This is the key to healing.

A favorite technique of mine is to remind myself what I love and appreciate about the person who triggered me. Another is to think of the trigger as a gift that allows me to look at myself and grow more emotionally aware. I remember when I learned this technique, the next time I was having a strong reaction, I began picturing the person that triggered me as a literal gift. Wrapping paper, bow, and all! It made me laugh and I was able to remind myself what I loved about them.

The next time you're triggered by someone, look at them from a different perspective—one of love and compassion. Notice how little time it takes you to shift your energy and get a sense of peace from this perspective.

Another technique for finding clarity is asking yourself questions. Here are some ideas of what you can ask:

- Do I want to be right?
- Am I blaming someone or something for my emotional pain?
- Am I comparing myself with another person?
- Am I complaining about someone else?
- Am I creating a story around my reaction?"

Our thoughts and beliefs form the story that creates our feelings, which then produce our actions, then our situation. What if you could change all that? Well, you can.

First, take these steps:
- Notice the physical sensations in your body, the painful ones.
- Notice what you are thinking.
- Feel those physical sensations without judgment; they are not good or bad.
- Try not to react to any painful emotions. If you need to, walk away until you can respond.
- Change your thoughts based on what you want to create.

Then:
- Notice when you have pleasant physical sensations in your body.
- Notice what you are thinking.
- Feel those physical sensations.
- Cultivate those.
- Respond from this place.

These techniques are powerful, but it does take practice to become proficient. I highly recommend starting to become more aware today. Over the course of a day, you will likely have several opportunities to practice noticing your feelings and thoughts without reacting, whether it's while driving, with a coworker, with your spouse, or at the grocery store.

During this process you may notice an increase of negative emotions about yourself as you become more aware of your feelings and reactions. I'd like to make it very clear how important it is to be gentle with yourself. Write these words on a piece of paper and remind yourself often. Without those words I would not be where I am today in my growth.

BE GENTLE WITH YOURSELF

Remember this is a journey, not a destination. The beauty of these tools is that you will be able to utilize them every day to create a more joy-filled life. You won't take everything so personally, you'll learn to have more fun, and you'll start creating your life instead of reacting to your life. You always have a choice. Which wolf are you going to feed—the angry, resentful wolf or the loving, compassionate one?

Our Stories

Susan's Story
Sisters Weekend Year Two, 1986 (Written in 2005)
Kentville Hotel, Hampton Beach, NH

I dug up some photos from this weekend to jog my memory. As I look through them, I think, "Who is this person?" Short dark hair, slumped shoulders, pale skin. A part of me feels sad when I look at these pictures… yet another part thinks of how far I've come.

I see us on the bed, a beer can in my hand. At the time, it seemed like a good idea. I could relax after a few beers. It had nothing to do with my sisters and everything to do with me. I loved my sisters. They were caring and fun to be with. I had a lot of internal issues, but I didn't know how to cope with all my feelings. That's just the way it was.

Looking at the pictures brings back memories of times when I didn't like myself much. It's okay to be able to say that now. I'm grateful I didn't blame my sisters for what I was feeling and didn't let my fears keep me home. I always thought if I stayed home, they would know something was wrong. That they would know something was wrong was scarier than just going and making the best of it.

Although it was not easy for me, something significant happened along the way: I began to change. I was not committed to my feelings of inferiority; I was committed to loving myself. It wasn't easy to share with my sisters how much I struggled to attend these weekends in the early years or so. However, not sharing was even more painful.

On our weekends, I often wouldn't engage in conversations. Instead, I would just sit and go into my head. I would wish I was at home in my comfort zone. My sister Michelle would notice and ask me what I was thinking about. I couldn't hide my sadness over not feeling like I had anything to contribute to the conversation, or that too many people were talking and I couldn't speak loud enough to be heard.

Once I started sharing how I felt, things began to change. I couldn't hide anymore. I had to challenge the feeling that I wasn't good enough. I did this by talking about and, more importantly, not acting on those thoughts. I could have believed them and stayed home, but that would also have been painful. So, I decided I would always show up, no matter if my thoughts told me I'd be happier staying home. I just kept showing up, despite the negative thoughts and uncomfortable emotions I was experiencing.

These things were life changing. The more I let go of the stories I was telling myself, the more I stepped into the whole experience of these beautiful weekends, and the more creative I became and inspired to embrace every experience. I found new ways of expressing myself. For example, I realized if I wanted to be heard, I could stand up to share something, instead of sitting. On shopping excursions, I would typically go into my head and complain that I hated shopping. However, in the spirit of opening myself to new ways of showing up, I decided I would embrace it and find ways to enjoy it! This was another way to step out of my comfort zone. I learned that participating, rather than disengaging and complaining, changed everything. Showing up in my life and being present is a gift I give to myself. These weekends, along with my loving sisters, have supported me deeply. It only gets better with each passing year!

Weekend after weekend, we shared more. We moved out of the superficial stage and began a somewhat turbulent, deepening stage. Bringing painful emotions to the surface can cause many different reactions and responses. The label of being the shyest, which I had since I was born, slowly faded. It took at least six or seven years for it to begin, and as things changed, I was able to relax and enjoy myself more fully on our weekends.

I now know quitting and withdrawing is not an option for me. I'm much more aware of when I wish to withdraw—and usually choose not to. Being committed to something healthy and authentic has sprouted seeds of joy, connection, and deep friendship with my sisters. If I had remained home, I would have been indulging my fears instead of experiencing the wonders of challenging them, staying committed, and spending time with my family.

Diane's Story
Sisters Weekend Year 5, 1989 (Written in 2005)
Days Inn Hyannis, MA

At the end of year five, I told myself I would not go on any more sisters weekends. Something was happening inside me, which started before I even left the house. I was anxious about going and I didn't know why. I know I was still figuring out how to be their sister instead of their mother. My instincts have always been to take care of my siblings. Being the oldest of ten children, my role has been a caregiver or mother to everyone. Now I was being told to stop. They wanted me to just be their sister. Everyone had grown up and started having their own families at this point. And I had mine.

When we arrived in Hyannis and started the weekend, I still felt uncomfortable. That year, we'd decided to extend the weekend into a four-day getaway. We spent much of the time around the pool trying to come up with a theme, dressing for that theme, or planning our next meal.

When we were doing birthday gifts, I decided to play a practical joke on Dolores and give her a bag of licorice. All the other years, our gift exchange had amounted to much more.

"What's the matter, Dolores?" I asked. "I thought you liked licorice?"

The look on her face said it all. Dolores tried to play it cool, and I tried to keep her guessing. Eventually I gave her real gift, but the momentum had been lost and the joke went bad. Dolores couldn't shake it off for most of the weekend.

I went on with more reactions to an emotion I still wasn't aware of. I chased Elaine around the hotel room with a needle to pop the pimple on her face. Elaine was scared, trying to get away from me. We were all laughing, but I don't think anyone thought it was funny.

During the day, we did some shopping and walking around, which was good because it kept us busy and away from each other. We're still not sure how it happened, but Michelle had a little too much to drink the night before the whale watch, our only planned event. Staying behind was not an option for her. I'm not sure if we saw any whales on that excursion; the energy was pretty drowned out at that point.

Amid some chaos and heavy emotions, Susan and Linda went to a store across the street and bought squirt guns. When they came back into the hotel room, they started squirting everyone. The sisters were screaming for them to stop. What a ruckus!

The whole weekend was filled with some damaging energy. It was like nothing we had ever experienced on a sisters weekend, but I think it was familiar from our childhoods. Jealousy, power struggles, and manipulation were the forefront runners that weekend. All of us have our little quirks, but this year took the cake.

I know that there were things my sisters did that bothered me, and I did things that bothered them as well. I think we all couldn't wait for the weekend to be over. In the end, we managed to finish the weekend with just the thoughts of not going on anymore.

But, lo and behold, the next year we went again.

Having a theme, planned events, and more space certainly makes a difference over being in two hotel rooms, all squished in, trying to keep our cool. This year is when we came up with the motto "always leave wanting more."

I do believe this year helped us realize that we had our own work to do before we could continue. And so it began growing…

Elaine's Story
Sisters Weekend Year 17, 2001 (Written in 2005)
Michelle's House, North Attleboro, MA

I was already anxious when we met that weekend, knowing what the topic of discussion would to be. Linda had spearheaded the agenda and decided we would all come with five things we liked about ourselves. I remember thinking, "How dare she ask us to do such a thing?"

I tried to make my list but could not for the life of me figure out what to write. The more I thought about it, the more anxious I became. I was angry with Linda for asking us to do this. My life was going well, but I had never given much thought to myself. I was still lost, though nobody could tell on the surface. I just went along, thinking all the bad things were behind me. So, why was it so hard to write five simple things I liked about myself? I wasn't a bad person. I had a good heart. I could love, laugh, cry, and give just as much as anyone else. But somewhere deep inside me, this monster lurked. I felt pain just thinking about answering that question.

I recall Linda asked me several times over the weekend if I was ready to share my list with everyone. I just wanted to pop her one. It felt like she was picking on me, like she had a plan to destroy everything I had become by asking me to share something I could not. You see, deep inside, I could not find anything about me I liked. I never felt worthy as a child; I was the one my mother picked on the most. I never got the attention I so hungrily sought.

I had spent years fighting for myself and what I believed in, but I never figured out what made me tick.

The morning of our last day, as we all sat around in Michelle's living room, a moment came that changed my life forever.

"Elaine," Linda said, "it's your turn to share the five things you like about yourself."

I'd been hoping she would forget, but somehow I knew Linda would not let up. Silence filled the room, and anxiety and anger boiled inside me. I couldn't escape this time. Linda was persistent. Somehow, she knew I had nothing to say but wanted to hear it. It felt cruel at the time. Now, I know it was for the best.

"Why didn't you come to sisters weekend at Dolores's beach house in 1997?" she asked.

Why was she demanding so much of me? At this point I just wanted out of that house, but I couldn't leave because Linda's car had me blocked in. Once I realized this, I came back inside and admitted my pain.

Twice over the years, I had made the conscious decision not to attend our sisters weekend. My sisters did not know the truth, but I did. I had suffered from feelings of inadequacy, rejection, and sorrow as a child and throughout most of my adult life. Allowing these feelings to come out of the closet caused so many mixed emotions among my sisters, I wasn't sure what was going on around me. I remember Diane wanting to hug me, as Diane always does. Somehow, this time, I did not want her hugs. Linda wanted me to keep talking, but I just wanted to leave. Michelle was reminded of some memories I was sharing while I let it all out that day.

At the age of twelve, I wanted attention so bad that I cut my wrists—just enough for them to bleed a little. Michelle was there in the kitchen when I came downstairs. It backfired because my mother couldn't help me; she was hurting inside, just like I was.

It didn't stop after I left the house and got married. My pain continued. I overcompensated through the years by working hard and trying my best to have a good life. What I realize now is that I was a classic co-dependent, people pleasing, enabler that based my feelings on making others happy. It did not serve me or my marriage well. Although my marriage lasted nineteen years, it was tumultuous, chaotic, and unhealthy. I was not able to embrace who I am or get to understand or love myself. Always seeking others approval and not getting it created a lot of pain. Little did I know, while going through marriage counseling for three years, I was growing. It started there.

The 2001 sisters weekend was the beginning of the end for me. I realized these weekends were not just about getting together and having fun. They had become a spiritual part of who we were as individuals and as a family. The bond we had developed could no longer be broken. Sharing my pain was cathartic for me. All that was broken was going to start to heal. I shared my pain and felt freer than I ever had, but my work had just begun.

My healing journey took far longer than I imagined it would. I needed many years of therapy and recovery work with a twelve-step program to get to the root of my pain. I can now say that I have the tools and the support I need to be emotionally healthy and make better choices. Sister weekends have helped me grow and learn to love myself. I no longer need others' approval. I can attend our annual weekends and have fun.

Michelle's Story
Sisters Weekend Year 18, 2002 (Written in 2005)
Elaine's House, Lakeville, MA

2002 marked the eighteenth year of our annual sisters weekends. I can't believe so many have passed. I'm so happy we're all still willing to spend quality time with each other.

Our weekends seem to be changing as the years go on. At first, they were about having fun and being without our kids or husbands. Now, our weekends are more about sharing and getting to know each other a little bit better.

The eighteenth year was different in many ways. First, I had been living in California for a year and a half, and both Dolores and I had to fly home to attend. It was not just the cost of the ticket I had to think about, but an eight-hour flight each way. But I thought about how I had started these weekends eighteen years ago and was committed to continuing them, no matter what it took. I couldn't miss one.

It was on this weekend that I found out our getaways weren't fun or easy for everyone. I always looked forward to them and never thought for a moment that they created fear for some of my sisters.

Susan informed me that this was the first year she did not have to take a Tylenol PM to fall asleep. That was a wake-up call for me. Not that I took it personally. Rather, it made me realize that it was difficult, uncomfortable, and maybe even painful for her to be around us for the weekend. It caused her so much anxiety. I had to wonder how many of my other sisters had felt the same about these weekends, for how long, and why.

Susan told us that it was her inner soul-searching that made her grow to the point she had reached that weekend, and she did not have those anxious feelings as often. This made me realize how committed she was. Our obligations to continue these weekends helped us grow and learn more about each other and ourselves.

I couldn't understand how some of my sisters felt because I never had those feelings of depression or anxiety. I lived my life moment to moment. Sure, I had some experiences that made me uncomfortable or sad, but I never stayed in that place; I always looked ahead. When my sisters would share their traumas or marital difficulties, I could be empathetic, but did not fully grasp their pain.

This is what these weekends are about—caring, growing, listening, and having fun!

We started the weekend by visiting our father's grave, planting flowers, and saying a prayer. We held hands in a circle, as we did most of our weekends, and said the Lord's Prayer. We then went to our father's best friend's funeral. For the rest of the weekend, we enjoyed the relaxing atmosphere Elaine set at her home. She made strawberries dipped in chocolate and had a warm, bubbling hot tub ready for us.

We had been sending emails back and forth for weeks before the getaway. Each morning, I looked forward to those emails and all the joking we did. Sometimes the anticipation is just as much fun as the weekend itself.

The theme for that weekend was to write what "togetherness" meant to each of us. Surprisingly, all our definitions were unique, but we agreed we felt the same about each other as a family and as friends.

Here's what I wrote:

> I really don't think any of you need to be reminded that I am the one that thought of sisters weekend, so we could spend time together. What togetherness means to me is spending time with my FAMILY.
> Family stands for:
> Father
> And
> Mother
> I
> Love
> You
>
> I believe we have mom and Dad to thank for such a special family. I know you have all heard me say time and time again the apple doesn't fall far from the tree. We are products of mom and Dad, who I feel are very special people. We were fortunate to have had them for our parents. They are the roots of our being.

I always thought when I was growing up that all the other families were luckier than me. I see now that they weren't. We have something that a lot of families don't have. We have friendship, love, and most of all respect for each other. This is all what brings us together. I love having six sisters I can call and talk to anytime I want. I know I can always count on each one of you in a time of need.

I think just the fact that we can spend a weekend together each year and still have the desire to do it the next year is something very special. Some families have trouble getting together for dinner.

We are seven individuals that are so diverse in some ways yet so much alike in other ways. We are all very sensitive, caring, strong willed and hardworking people. I value my relationship with each one of you.

You are all my sisters but also my best friends. I love you all.'

I'd like to share Elaine's letter as well:

Togetherness with my sisters is one of the most precious of all gifts. There is always joy in my heart when I think of the time, we share. The bond we have is one of love, laughter, and tears. I am so lucky to have such special sisters to bond and share my life's journey with. You are all a gift from God and treasured every day in your own special way. I can't imagine what life would have been like without each one of you. As we are together this weekend, I add another chapter to my book of precious moments. Memories are the heart and spirit of our lives to savor and reflect upon in the years to come.

With all my love always,
Elaine

We ended the weekend the same way we had begun: we held hands in a circle and said a prayer for each other. This weekend was a breakthrough for all of us, and I realized there truly is no place like home.

Marianne's Story
Sisters Weekend Year 18, 2002 (Written in 2005)
Lakeville, MA

The greatly anticipated eighteenth sisters weekend happened over Memorial Day weekend and was a two-way struggle for me. It took place at Elaine's beautiful, welcoming home, and my sisters and I spent a great deal of time motivating each other before the weekend began. We would email each other daily to plan the menu and events—who would cook, clean, or do nothing at all. We would eat marinated steak tips, grilled shrimp and vegetables, salad, and much more. There were a lot of laughs discussing what we would wear—or not wear, for that matter. A battle brewed over whether bikinis should be allowed in the hot tub and whether thong underwear should be allowed at all. We learned who of us could cook and who could not. Elaine never knew that I was one of the could-nots.

Most often, I would receive these emails at work, but sometimes they would go to my home email address. My husband would get angry and ask me to tell them not to send them to that one. It was a struggle to convince him to ignore them; he would not let it go. So, even though I was supposed to be happy, I was not. It felt like I was doing something wrong by leaving him to go on my special weekend.

The days leading up to the trip were challenging. My husband and I were struggling to communicate and argued over everything. Was it because it was a holiday weekend? Was it because he had to take care of the children while I was gone? I couldn't wait to be together with my all sisters in one place for forty-eight hours. I hadn't seen Dolores or Michelle since Christmas, yet I could not show my excitement at home.

When the moment came for me to leave my house, I was depressed and scared. I drove to my mother's house to meet my sisters but realized I had left with only twenty dollars in my pocket. I didn't want to go back and get more, too afraid of what my husband and I would say to each other. I held back tears and contemplated turning back to fix the problem with my marriage. I'm not sure why I kept going.

When I arrived, all the girls were already there. My emotions were high. I couldn't help but cry, knowing I was safe with them, happy to be together again.

I'm always learning new things from and about my sisters. They were all trying to heal and educate themselves while I always thought I was okay just the way I was. My life and marriage were not perfect, but I never thought I was in trouble. That weekend opened my eyes. I noticed how much my sisters were changing, and they were happier and more open. It was time to educate myself and learn how to be a better me. I couldn't change others, but I could change myself. Learning to love myself was a new priority. I was learning from Linda and Susan, who spent many moments that weekend sharing their feelings and educating the rest of us on how they'd begun to heal their inner selves. I listened intently, as if I were reaching out to a higher power. I wanted to learn how to heal my inner child, be more charitable, be a better mother and wife, and much more. Let the journey begin!

"What goes around comes around" is quite a true statement. If I was kind to others, they would be kind in return. I decided to be kinder at home than I had ever been. I wanted to treat my husband and children with respect, just as I treated all the other people in my life. Not that I was a mean person, just overly responsible. I was the one who couldn't break the rules, working hard to finish my college degree and grow my career. I worried about everything, carried the whole family's burdens on my shoulders, and took life way too seriously. I needed to change that part of me, relax a little, and take time to be gentle with myself and others. That's what I was learning from my sisters.

I was afraid to go home when the weekend was over. I didn't know what would become of my relationship with my husband. Linda gave me the best advice I'd ever received: "Walk into your home with love and trust and leave fear and doubt behind you." She coached me on a few easy statements that would help me make the first move with love and kindness. The baby steps I took to be a better person at home proved to be the same steps I needed to create a stronger and happier marriage. Using kind words such as *please* and *thank you* worked wonders for us. I've begun to read educational books on self-improvement and share my experiences with other people. The journey to healing myself and not blaming others has started as well.

Linda's Story
Sisters Weekend Year 19, 2003 (Written in 2005)
On Cranberry Pond, Middleboro, MA

I really did not know what to expect on our sisters weekend that year. The year before was nearly perfect, and I wasn't sure if it would be better or just different. So, I went with an open mind, relishing the thought of a full body massage, manicure, pedicure, and facial. The theme for the year was "it's all about me." Instead of buying gifts for each other, we had to buy one for ourselves. I struggled with this; it was hard for me to spend money on myself. I ended up buying myself a pair of twenty-dollar sunglasses. That was in my comfort zone.

When we arrived, I was surprised by how big the bed-and-breakfast was and the number of rooms it had. We met Jeannine, our hostess for the weekend, and while we were getting our luggage from the car, she mentioned it would be a busy weekend and we must get started. I thought I would die! What did she mean we were going to be busy? We had our own agenda; were we going to be separated all weekend, or have time for everything we wanted to do? I quashed my fears by telling myself, "Whatever will be, will be—and it will all work out for the best."

I was the first to have a manicure and pedicure, which was supposed to take two hours. I invited my sisters to visit me while I was being pampered if they weren't busy with their own spa treatments. After about fifteen minutes, a few of them came in. I had been telling the manicurist Joanne our story, and she had talked about her relationship (or lack thereof) with her only sister. Well, the conversation changed, and we spent the rest of the time chatting. My sisters came and went, and it ended up being so much fun. We had never shared so much of our weekend with a total stranger before. On our sisters weekends, we tended to stay close and not allow others into our circle. It was fun to share ourselves and what we do with others, in the hope it would help them with their relationships.

I learned more about myself that year than any other I can remember at that point. I had been learning about reaction vs. response and emotional awareness, so I'd been practicing for a while. At the beginning of the weekend, the discussion of facial expressions came up. Several sisters make faces (reacting) instead of speaking, which I discovered triggers others. I am one of the sisters who shows my feelings on my face. What I did not realize is that everyone else noticed them too. It scared me that people could see what I was feeling. I wanted to be more aware of that so I could change.

During parts of the weekend, I began to experience emotional pain and wasn't sure why. I was with my six best friends, yet my heart hurt. What was up with that? So, I decided to take the time to feel the pain, to try to figure out what was bothering me. What I felt was anger and resentment. I noticed I was judging my sisters and it did not feel good. I narrowed it down to the fact that I thought some of them weren't growing, and I wanted them to so they could be happier. I didn't understand what was holding them back. I had been working on myself for ten years at that point, and it felt so good (most of the time) to break the behavior patterns that kept me sad and depressed. I wanted that for all of us. The lesson I had to learn is you cannot change others; they must want to change. But not everyone was ready to do the work.

I knew that the things you dislike about someone else are usually a reflection of yourself, and realized I was looking in the wrong direction. I was the one not growing like I wanted to, but was too busy trying to see if my sisters were changing. Comparison is not a healthy way to live. Everyone was in a different place, and I needed to respect that. I already knew that, but I wasn't practicing it! That's when I realized I needed to stay focused on my own growth, not others'. I was thankful for the opportunity to be more aware. That's how you grow, one experience at a time. If you don't learn the lesson the first time, you'll be given another opportunity and another until you get it!

Dolores's Story
Sister Weekend Year 20, 2004 (Written in 2005)
Martha's Vineyard, Falmouth, MA

We were sitting in The Black Dog restaurant in Martha's Vineyard, perusing the menu, laughing, and talking. I'd lived in St. Charles, Illinois, for three years, and I complained about the lack of seafood options a lot. My eyes were bigger than my stomach, and I wanted everything on the menu that came from the ocean. When I spotted the little necks appetizer, I was delighted. I declared that I was getting an order and would not be sharing with anyone.

Everyone but Elaine seemed fine with that. She expressed some disappointment and even implied I was being selfish. I told her I didn't get little necks in Illinois, and the serving size was enough for me to eat. Heck, I could probably have eaten two. I tried to focus on what the others were saying, but my history with Elaine went so deep I couldn't shake it off.

My anxiety continued even after we left the restaurant and started shopping. I wasn't really enjoying myself. I needed to know what she was thinking about me.

We ended up in an ice cream parlor called Mad Martha's—a famous spot in the Vineyard. We had to gather at different tables due to the size of our group, and as we ate, Susan asked what we thought our relationships would be like if we hadn't started sister weekends. Elaine responded first. She pointed at me and said we would probably still hate each other.

That was it: all I needed to be sent into one of the worst panic attacks I've ever had. My fear and doubt took over in a very real, very physical way. When we finished our ice cream, I left the parlor and went into a nearby store. Thank goodness I had a water bottle with me because I was having such trouble breathing and controlling my emotions. I was shaking and crying. My head was telling me Elaine hated me, and my heart was agreeing.

When I finally got my emotions under control, I sought Linda for comfort and support. She knew I was in pain but didn't try to comfort me. Instead, she said we would address it later. Of course, that was not enough for me. When we left the store, I wanted to test if what I'd felt was true. Did Elaine hate me? I would only know from the way she reacted to me.

I walked by a store window that she was looking into and saw some stained-glass ornaments. Earlier in the trip, she had told me she was looking for something just like them, so I pointed them out to her, but she didn't seem interested. This seemed to validate my feelings.

As we continued to shop, I thought all my sisters except Linda were oblivious to what was going on. How could they not see the pain I was in? We had some time before we had to take the ferry back, so a few girls continued shopping and the rest of us waited at the dock. Linda, Susan, Marianne, Elaine, and I sat along a stone wall. We passed the time by discussing our book, but I was still in a lot of pain and holding back the tears as best I could. Quietly, I told Susan I was disappointed she hadn't noticed. My thoughts were so negative, I made up my mind to never come back for another sisters weekend, nor would I help write the book.

When we got back to the bed-and-breakfast, I retreated to my room to pull myself together. It was then I decided I had choices. Was I going to address this pain or not? I was really scared. I was scared to stay and scared to leave. Fight or flight instinct came naturally to me. They were my survival, and I acted on those instincts regularly. Either way the weekend could not end for me in that kind of pain. I managed to create enough time and space to consider my choices. I had to change my thoughts; "I'm hated," "I will never be good enough," "why me?" I knew I had the support of my other sisters whether they were aware of my anxiety or not. How could it possibly get any worse? If an opportunity presented itself, I was going to act on it.

We ordered pizza for dinner, and I ended up at the table with Elaine and Michelle. When Elaine left to get something to drink, an opportunity presented itself. I warned Michelle that I was going to tell Elaine about what I had been feeling and I was sorry for putting her in this awkward situation.

When Elaine sat down, I simply asked her, "Do you love me?"

Before I could blink, she had flown out of her chair and landed in my lap. She hugged me and told me how much she loves me. I just sobbed in her arms. The rest of the sisters weren't quite sure what was happening, but they didn't intervene or question it. I was so happy. I had my sister back. I felt complete, free from our past.

I left this sisters weekend feeling I had addressed my concerns with Elaine and made a responsible choice about the pain I'd been experiencing.

But there was more—much more.

Months later, when I decided this would be a great story for the "letting go" chapter of our book, I felt like I needed Elaine's input. I wanted her memories of the weekend, and even her approval before I wrote it. Did I need to hear her version of that day? Would the story be incomplete without it? I soon realized that even though it was wonderful to have addressed my feelings, it was me and only me who had created what happened on that day. Nothing Elaine said or did caused the emotional rollercoaster I experienced. It was my own insecurities about our relationship. "Does she love me? Does she hate me? Does she approve of what I'm saying or dong?" These anxieties formed that pain. Elaine and I had had this pattern almost our whole lives. When was I going to break that cycle? I was tired of the painful emotional rollercoaster.

I realized I will never be happy if I rely on others' perceptions of me, seeking what I did not receive as a child. Being rebellious and trying to please others were my way of owning my power, but it wasn't working for me anymore.

I am eternally grateful that I challenged my fear that day. I now look at my relationships with everyone around me in a different way. I'm working on letting go of blaming others for the way I feel and the insecurities that create those painful emotions. But most importantly, I am learning to let go of the past and choosing instead to be grateful for today. I truly do love, respect, and admire all my sisters.

Mom's Story
Written by Loretta Ethier in 2005

I want to start by saying that I wasn't the best mother at times. Nobody teaches you the rules of being a mother. You try to learn from your mistakes. My husband was an alcoholic, which meant we were far from being a normal family. I would get frustrated with him and take it out on the kids. It wasn't until I went to an Al-Anon meeting that I learned what to do and what not to do. But that didn't' happen until maybe fifteen years into the marriage and ten children later.

My children didn't have a normal childhood. They learned how to be responsible at an early age. I had to go to work to make ends meet and the kids were often left alone. I tried to teach them as much as I could, but it wasn't always enough. Thank God for the family that came to our rescue in times of need. As for each individual child, they are all unique, lovable, and responsible.

Mom and Dad

Our parents were not always ideal role models, and we had to live with those repercussions. Our healing started once Dad started living an alcohol-free life, after years of using it to numb the pain of his own childhood trauma. Mom went to Al-Anon to learn how to deal with Dad's alcoholism and Dad went to Alcoholics Anonymous. Some of us younger kids went to Alateen to learn about the behaviors we lived with and how to deal with them. It was a good start, knowing there were support groups to help us understand how to survive in a dysfunctional family.

Mom and Dad were also an integral part of our mission to grow and stay close over the years. Despite the dysfunction, when they knew better, they did better. When they were finally able to improve their own emotional health, they taught us how to love unconditionally. We didn't always practice these lessons, but we did the best we could at the time. To this day, Mom still loves each of us equally.

They both helped us grow in their own way. Dad, by challenging his addiction. Mom, by her strength and commitment to living in the present and always helping others. Our mom never gave up or gave in. She had the faith of a saint. Even today as she lives in a nursing home with dementia, she exhibits the true meaning of unconditional love to all of us and those around her. She may not be able to articulate our names, but she feels the love and shows her love.

When Dad challenged his addiction, he grew as well. There were a few years when one of my brothers was mad at him and the family. He kept himself and his children away from us. Another sibling said to Dad, "Nine out of ten kids talking to you isn't bad." Dad said, "That's not good enough. I want all ten of my children in my life." He loved us all and had a special relationship with each of us. Dad had a fifth-grade education, but the mind of an engineer. He invented surround sound in our living room ceiling back in the eighties, as well as an answering machine before those were a thing.

Mom and Dad loved that we had our annual sisters weekends, and supported our efforts. They both influenced our growth as we watched them transform their lives once the addiction was addressed. Amazingly enough, we started our weekends the year after Dad became sober. Initially, we would start our gatherings by meeting at our family home before carpooling to our destination. Dad would give us each twenty dollars for the trip. (In 1985 that was a lot of money to us.) Mom would write us personalized or group letters and tell us to read them over the weekend. The love was unconditional.

Our Stories

Where We Are Today

In 2020, we were not able to physically be together because of the COVID-19 pandemic. On top of that, our mother's dementia was progressing. She needed twelve-hour-a-day care, camera supervision at night, and someone in her house that could intervene in emergencies.

Although we didn't have our sisters weekend, what we did have was a group of well-intentioned women—the seven sisters—caring for their mother. We put together a support schedule, bought groceries, maintained the yard, cleaned the house, did the laundry, kept track of doctors' appointments, and more. All seven sisters showed up with so much love and compassion in their hearts, and they grew and grew. It was a full year of connection and support, not only for our mother but ourselves and each other.

We learned even more valuable lessons while caring for our mom. The most significant for me was to not expect anything from anyone. The less I expected, the more I received. Not everyone was able to help make a schedule to fit mom's needs, at first. As time went on, some sisters and brothers asked if there was a way for them to help. They offered to go over one evening a week to make dinner or take an extra shift so a primary caregiver could have some time off. Everything always worked out for us, when we let go of the outcome and allowed everyone to make their own decisions.

> *"Life is not linear, but neither is it circular. It's a spiral. And as we grow, we notice the same things come around, but we see them from a higher perspective or with a deeper understanding."*
> —Russell Brand

Year thirty-seven of our sisters weekends was one for the books! It was June 2021, and we decided to include Elaine, who had opted out of the last ten sisters weekends. She was learning about her triggers and needed time and space to get through the process. There was some fear about including her because the last time Elaine had attended, the weekend was filled with triggers and strong reactions toward each of us. We were in New Hampshire and only had two cars. It was a long drive home for those sharing the car with her. So, what was different this year? We all had to challenge any fears we still had. Was she ready? Would she get triggered and ruin the weekend? At this point in our lives, we all wanted peace and harmony, not more drama. I believed with all my heart that she was ready to return to our weekends and would not get triggered. And if she did, I would hand her the car keys and send her on her way! But I didn't need to.

We didn't discuss the past; it was irrelevant. Living in the present was all we could do. That was where our power was. We preplanned and set intentions. We had done our work, just as she had done hers. We all were ready to make it happen, and it did!

I sent out a group text to ask who was in for the sisters weekend, and Elaine was the first person to respond! The rest of the sisters chimed in, and within two hours we had a house booked and a weekend planned in Mystic, Connecticut.

Once we arrived with all our paraphernalia, food, and gifts, we settled into our beautiful rental home with a large deck. It was a far cry from where we started thirty-seven years ago! We gathered in a circle, set our intentions, and said a prayer. Elaine started the gift-giving early. She shared letters she had written to each of us that expressed what she admired, paired with a quote that could be put on the wall. She even wrote a letter to herself, sharing her journey and her growth over the last ten years.

The weekend continued flawlessly, with gift-giving and a scavenger hunt downtown. We had a visit from a cousin who lived nearby, lots of laughter; there was a deep sense of presence among us. Some of us walked in the mornings, pairing off to have private conversations. Other times, we talked as a group. We cooked together and shared our accomplishments from over the last year.

It ended with us holding hands in a circle, as most of our weekends started and ended. Elaine thanked us for inviting her back into our weekends. We all agreed that although she had not been with us physically, she was always in our hearts. She had even participated unknowingly by calling or texting one of us while we were away.

Everything is always evolving. What worked one year may not work another year. As we grow and expand, so do our weekends.

The gift of sisterhood is deeply satisfying, as is knowing the unconditional love and support we have for one another in good times and bad.

Our Stories

The Ethier Girls - September 4, 2021
Dolores, Michelle, Susan, Diane, Elaine, Marianne, and Linda.

Your Weekends

Now that you've heard our stories and how we had to overcome trauma to grow, I'd like to share with you some more practical advice on how to plan for a weekend of your own!

- Have a Plan
- Pick a date.
- How much can everyone easily afford?
- Where to stay?
- What to bring?
- Decide on a theme if you want one.
- Figure Out the Cost

It's likely that each sister will have different financial situations and money mindsets. This can cause some anxiety, feelings of inadequacy, or other painful emotions. Recognize your feelings about money as another opportunity to look at yourself and see what keeps you separate from your sisters. Jealousy over income can cause someone to withdraw or not want to join the sisters weekend. Don't try to change anyone's money story before the event. Recognize it and make it work so everyone can join in without the fear of not having enough.

Costs:
- Lodging (if you are not staying at someone's house)
- Gas
- Food
- Props
- Gifts
- Drinks
- Going out to eat
- Entertainment (play, museum, movie, etc.)
- Shopping

First pick dates that work for everyone, then decide on a location. Once that's done, you can add other details to your weekend getaway—like food, activities, themes, and props if needed.

Decide beforehand what you want to create in this time together, how you want it to look, and especially how you want to feel. Remember, everyone in the group has different ideas and perspectives. One person may love details and will bring a ton of props for your theme, while another may not. Someone may be a minimalist and have a reaction to all the stuff someone else brings. Learn to accept the differences and embrace them. (We had to! Diane brought so much stuff and then had to spend the whole weekend organizing it all.)

Food can be easy. Cooking on the grill is always an uncomplicated choice, as is eating out or ordering in. Don't make food an issue. Everyone could bring what they like for snacks. One sister may bring breakfast foods and someone else may bring dinner food. You get to decide based on where you're staying and who likes to cook.

Are there any foods from your childhood that bring back happy memories? Bringing those may help make the weekend an enjoyable bonding experience. Our favorites are licorice, orange peanuts, and Thin Mints.

Let's Sort It Out

Everything is flexible, depending on your plan. Including some entertainment adds cost but creates memories. Gifts can have a spending limit if you want to do gifts. Window shopping is always fun, but it's nice to bring some money to spend on a trinket or two.

My sisters and I always do a kitty when we arrive. Everyone puts in a pre-determined amount of money, and we use that to go out to eat. One year, a sister did not have any money to give. Even so, we all supported her. We didn't judge her or try to fix the situation. We understood that she couldn't pay for anything, and the rest of us took care of it for her.

Depending on the number of people, you need to decide what type of space you want: hotel, Airbnb, camping, glamping, or someone's house if they have the space (and can get rid of any family members that live there).

Be creative, and don't get attached to a single destination. It's not where you go, it's how you feel and what you do that makes the weekend rich!

That said, staying at someone's home to keep the cost down does not lessen the weekend's value. It can be just as fun and sometimes even more relaxed and easy! Just remember that the person hosting should not be the only one cleaning up or making plans. It's always a joint effort. Everyone needs to bring something to the weekend for it to be meaningful. You need to meet people where they are. Not everyone has the same amount of creativity or number of ideas. This changes as we evolve as people.

Emotional Preparedness

One of the most important parts of the weekend is preparing for it emotionally. Set an intention and hold that in your heart. For example, your intention may be to bond with your sisters, create new memories, and learn something new about them over the weekend.

Keep your eye on your own growth and happiness; they will take you places you never dreamed of. Be gentle with yourself and those around you. Everything takes practice. Learn to love yourself. Take time between these annual trips to get to know yourself and your beliefs. Consider reading some self-help books, taking a course, or joining a group that can guide you with a relatable process.

What We Learned and How You Can Prepare

- Have a theme.
- Be flexible.
- Drop all labels from your childhood.
- Try to live in the moment.
- Buy gifts.
- Plan meals and cook together.
- Practice meeting everyone where they are on their journey.
- Share your talents and gifts.
- Let each other be who they are.
- Look for the best qualities in each other.
- Talk about the past, but do not dwell on it.
- It's okay if someone doesn't want to come to the yearly celebration.
- Add music to your time together.
- Trust yourselves and each other.
- Share your strengths.
- Recognize your weaknesses and work on them.
- Learn to take responsibility for yourselves and your feelings.
- Do not be attached to the outcome.

The next sections have some questions to ask yourself to see what would inspire you to commit to a weekend with your family or friends. There are also questions about yourself and what triggers you into a reaction. These are to help you delve into your own journey of self-awareness. Getting to know yourself is the healthiest way to make your life happier, whether you choose to go on weekends or not.

Two Questions to Ask Yourself

- Why do you want to go on a weekend with your sister(s)? Be as specific as you can.
- What do you want this weekend to look or feel like? Be as specific as you can.

Becoming Aware/More Questions

I'd like to preface these questions by noting that their purpose is to help you become more aware of your thoughts and how they create your feelings and then ultimately your results. With this, you can decide what you want to create in the long term. These questions can be answered from all areas of your life, not just for family relationships.

- What triggers you? Make a list.
- Who triggers you? Make a list.
- How do you feel when you are triggered? (Angry, sad, confused, unlovable, etc.)
- How do you react when you are triggered? Write as many examples as you can. (Shout, withdraw, shop, use substances, cry, complain, etc.)
- How do you want to respond when triggered? Write as many examples as you can. (With clarity, relaxed, compassionately, etc.)
- Is there a specific belief, story, or traumatic event from your past that is causing you to be triggered? Example: Were you lied to by someone you loved and trusted and now you have become distrustful? Write the story and see if it can be changed. The past does not equal the future.
- How do you feel when you take responsibility for your actions and reactions?
- If you do react, what can you learn from it? What are your results from reacting? (Do you create distance, shut down, make unhealthy choices?)
- How can you respond instead of reacting?
- What is the outcome when you respond? This question is important to get clarity on what you are creating. (Create more intimacy, gain trust, make yourselves happier, etc.)

The Journey

My sisters and I have changed our story and broken the cycle we grew up in. Healing from our traumas has helped us create more memories with our mom and each other, instead of staying stuck in the pain of the past. We have tools that we continue to use today. It was hard for us sometimes, no doubt. Painful emotions came up for each of us. Without those moments, we wouldn't have grown ourselves or our relationships. We would not be who we are or as close as we are today. Having adversity in our lives encouraged us to search for more meaning.

We've been successful because we did the work. We became more aware of our emotions, patterns, triggers, passions, and joys. It would have been so easy to say, "Eff this! I'm not doing it anymore!" But we didn't want that. We wanted to create a safe place to share our feelings; be who we are; learn not to judge, blame, or feel jealous; and have fun doing it. We allowed room for the emotions that came up whenever they did—and they will always come up. We cannot always control the emotions, but we can control our responses. We "held the space" for sisters when they couldn't participate fully or were in pain. We experimented and planned our weekends based on what we learned year to year.

We want to encourage all of you to connect with your family and friends on a deeper level. Don't let fears and triggers break you apart. Heal yourselves by learning to love yourselves. Don't allow trauma to define you. You get to choose.

Choose wisely.

Recommended Reading:

Waking The Tiger: Healing Trauma by Peter Levine

The Body Keeps the Score: Brain, Mind, and Body in the Healing of Trauma by Bessel van der Kolk, M.D.

Myofascial Release, Healing Ancient Wounds by John F. Barnes, P.T.

The Seat of the Soul by Gary Zukav

Made in United States
North Haven, CT
07 February 2023